"The greatest strength of this [book?] [is the] clear way Madueme respects [the inter]actions between Christianity and science. He rightly notes that the warfare depiction of their relationship has been rejected by historians of science for decades. Where there are conflicts, they by no means characterize the main ways faith and science have rightly interacted for centuries. This is a must-read, if for no other reason than how it debunks the standard narrative about alleged conflicts between Christianity and science, such as the Galileo affair and the Scopes Trial. Madueme knows his stuff, and I highly recommend this book."

J. P. Moreland, Distinguished Professor of Philosophy, Biola University

"As the myth of warfare between science and religion resurges in our culture, many find themselves caught up in disputes over everything from climate to vaccines to evolution. This book may surprise you with its far-ranging review of the complex, often mutualistic relationship between theology and science. Madueme offers a fruitful way of relating science and faith."

Todd Charles Wood, Founder and President, Core Academy of Science

"Here's a helpful book that is also fun to read. Hans Madueme explains the relationship between faith and science with wit and humility. More importantly, he directs our awe and amazement of creation to its proper aim—to worship of the Creator."

Kenneth Keathley, Research Professor of Theology, Southeastern Baptist Theological Seminary; author, *Faith and Science: A Primer for a Hypernatural World*

"What an attractive book! It's brief, highly readable, and full of carefully deployed knowledge. Hans Madueme speaks to many kinds of people, from young Christians puzzled by the alleged hostility between faith and science to inquirers wondering whether the Christian faith shows intellectual virtue. Well worth your time!"

C. John Collins, Professor of Old Testament, Covenant Theological Seminary; author, *Science and Faith: Friends or Foes?*

"Hans Madueme provides an irenic and evenhanded account of the common approaches to understanding the relationship between science and religious belief. In answer to his question 'Does science make God irrelevant?,' he gives a resounding *no!* I highly recommend this short introduction to an important subject."

Stephen C. Meyer, Director, Discovery Institute's Center for Science and Culture; author, *Return of the God Hypothesis*

"Today, a destructive narrative permeates our culture and the church: Science and Christianity are at odds. Highly respected theologian Hans Madueme effectively challenges this false narrative. Having spent years working at the frontier of the science-faith conversation, he is well suited to remind us of the role Christianity played in the origin of modern science. By presenting the reader with the appropriate theological and philosophical frameworks, he ably guides us to the conclusion that Christianity fully harmonizes with science."

Fazale "Fuz" Rana, biochemist; President and CEO, Reasons to Believe

Does Science Make God Irrelevant?

TGC Hard Questions
Jared Kennedy, Series Editor

Did the Resurrection Really Happen?, Timothy Paul Jones
Does God Care about Gender Identity?, Samuel D. Ferguson
Does Science Make God Irrelevant?, Hans Madueme
Is Christianity Good for the World?, Sharon James
What Does Depression Mean for My Faith?, Kathryn Butler, MD
Where Is God in a World with So Much Evil?, Collin Hansen
Why Do We Feel Lonely at Church?, Jeremy Linneman

Does Science Make God Irrelevant?

Hans Madueme

WHEATON, ILLINOIS

Does Science Make God Irrelevant?

© 2025 by Hans Madueme

Published by Crossway
        1300 Crescent Street
        Wheaton, Illinois 60187

All rights reserved. No part of this publication may be reproduced, stored in a retrieval system, or transmitted in any form by any means, electronic, mechanical, photocopy, recording, or otherwise, without the prior permission of the publisher, except as provided for by USA copyright law. Crossway® is a registered trademark in the United States of America.

Cover design: Ben Stafford

Cover images: Unsplash

First printing 2025

Printed in the United States of America

Unless otherwise indicated, Scripture quotations are from the ESV® Bible (The Holy Bible, English Standard Version®), © 2001 by Crossway, a publishing ministry of Good News Publishers. Used by permission. All rights reserved. The ESV text may not be quoted in any publication made available to the public by a Creative Commons license. The ESV may not be translated in whole or in part into any other language.

Scripture quotation marked NIV is taken from the Holy Bible, New International Version®, NIV®. Copyright © 1973, 1978, 1984, 2011 by Biblica, Inc.™ Used by permission of Zondervan. All rights reserved worldwide. www.zondervan.com. The "NIV" and "New International Version" are trademarks registered in the United States Patent and Trademark Office by Biblica, Inc.™

Trade paperback ISBN: 978-1-4335-9797-8
ePub ISBN: 978-1-4335-9799-2
PDF ISBN: 978-1-4335-9798-5

Library of Congress Cataloging-in-Publication Data
Names: Madueme, Hans, 1975– author.
Title: Does science make God irrelevant? / Hans Madueme.
Description: Wheaton, Illinois : Crossway, 2025. | Series: TGC hard questions | Includes bibliographical references and index.
Identifiers: LCCN 2024038937 (print) | LCCN 2024038938 (ebook) | ISBN 9781433597978 (trade paperback) | ISBN 9781433597985 (pdf) | ISBN 9781433597992 (epub)
Subjects: LCSH: Science and religion. | Christianity.
Classification: LCC BL239 .M35 2025 (print) | LCC BL239 (ebook) | DDC 261.5/5—dc23/eng/20250103
LC record available at https://lccn.loc.gov/2024038937
LC ebook record available at https://lccn.loc.gov/2024038938

Crossway is a publishing ministry of Good News Publishers.

BP		34	33	32	31	30	29	28	27	26	25
15	14	13	12	11	10	9	8	7	6	5	4	3	2	1

Contents

Does Science Make God Irrelevant? *1*

Notes *67*

Recommended Resources *79*

Scripture Index *83*

A GROWING NUMBER OF PEOPLE believe the earth is flat. No one knows exactly how many people share this belief, but a recent survey showed that 10 percent of 1,134 respondents believe the earth is flat—with 9 percent unsure.[1] In 2017, the American rapper B.o.B started a GoFundMe page to prove flat-earth theory by launching a satellite into space. That same year, NBA player Kyrie Irving made waves in a podcast interview defending a flat-earth cosmology. He later recanted and explained how viewing too much YouTube brainwashed him. You can roll your eyes, but an alarming number of people have been converted to a flat-earth view through YouTube disinformation.[2]

Surely most readers[3] will agree that flat-earthism is preposterous ("absolute bonkers," my son would say). You're probably not a flat-earther, but if you are an evangelical Christian, you may share some of that view's skepticism about contemporary science. If you are older, you have seen popular scientific advice about healthy eating, for example, change over the years. At one time, doctors told us low-fat diets reduce heart disease, but now they think some fats have health benefits. Same with eggs—first they were unhealthy; now nutritionists tell us they are healthy. Maybe you have thought, "Scientists change their mind about almost everything if you wait long enough." In light of how issues have been politicized in North America, many religious people are skeptical about climate change, and in a post-COVID world, Christians concerned about government overreach are often vaccine-skeptical, too.

The trouble with our skepticism is that if we are not careful, we can adopt a warfare understanding of the relationship between science and Christianity. Ironically, the atheist Jerry Coyne reflects the same attitude in his bestselling book *Faith vs. Fact: Why Science and Religion Are Incompatible*. The title tells you what he thinks about religious beliefs. Right from the preface, he pulls no punches: "Faith may be a gift in religion," he writes, "but in science it's poison, for faith is no way to find truth."[4] Coyne pits science and faith against each other, on opposite sides of the fence. Yes, believers reject his atheism, but we are often tempted to fight the same battle. Coyne fights for science, we might say, and we fight for faith.

DOES SCIENCE MAKE GOD IRRELEVANT?

Sadly, parents and churches can respond to this perceived war between science and faith by shielding young people from any serious interaction with mainstream science. They recognize that some scientific beliefs contradict what the Bible says about God and the world we live in, so they shut down their kids' interaction with secular science altogether. While sincere, this protective approach can backfire. It sets up young people who grow to love science as adults to be skeptical about their childhood faith later in life. At the other extreme, many non-Christians like Coyne agree Christianity and science will always be irreconcilable. The biblical view of origins doesn't count as genuine knowledge, they say, because it opposes empirical science. What's more, Scripture is full of supernatural events that cannot be proved scientifically: at best, science is agnostic about a world where miracles happen; at worst, science denies such a world exists.

I wrote this book for young Christians who love Jesus *and* science. Our society keeps telling you science and faith can't get along, but deep down you hope for an evangelical faith that takes science seriously. My aim in this book is to show you why that hope is entirely justified. Science and faith are intimate friends. The book unfolds in four steps: (1) criticizing the contemporary idea that science and faith have always been enemies, (2) explaining how Christian assumptions make science possible, (3) clarifying the perceived tension between science and miracles in the Bible, and (4) illustrating some ways faith and science can coexist as allies. By the end of the book, I hope you will be able to see how good science glorifies God.

Debunking the War between Science and Faith

Many of us grew up believing science and faith are at war. We absorbed this belief by cultural osmosis. We imagined theology and science on two ends of the spectrum, as enemies in mortal combat. The Joker versus Batman. Sherlock versus Moriarty. Science versus theology. The secular forces lined up on one side; the angels of light, on the other. This is a civil war, a battle to the death, and may the best man win.

We often think about Galileo's life in terms of this battle narrative.[5] Here was a great scientist surrounded by Bible-thumping fundamentalists who believed in geocentrism, the idea that the sun revolves around the earth. Galileo (1564–1642) proved the opposite—heliocentrism—and wrote books defending this truth. His reward? He was captured by the Roman Inquisition, tortured, and then sent to jail, where he spent the rest of his life in disgrace.

If you believe this, I have an oceanfront property in Iowa to sell you! This picture of Galileo is largely a myth; the true story is far more complex. First, Nicolaus Copernicus (1473–1543) and Johannes Kepler (1571–1630) originally had the idea; they gave serious defenses of heliocentrism long before Galileo. Second, some church leaders, including the pope, were initially sympathetic to Galileo's views. But we often forget that even in 1615 when Galileo went to Rome to defend his views to the Catholic Church, there was no definitive *proof* heliocentrism was correct (that came decades later with Isaac Newton). Many astronomers and physicists at the time disagreed with Galileo, because other models of the solar system made equally good sense of the data. Galileo's view wasn't the only available theory. At that point in history, it was perfectly rational for astronomers and church officials to disagree with Galileo.

The main alternative position was the geocentrism of Aristotle's cosmology, which the Catholic Church had fully embraced for centuries. Aristotle had become the foundation for Italy's moral and social fabric. If Galileo was right, *then beloved Aristotle was wrong*. In the seventeenth century, those were fighting words. That's probably why a Roman Catholic cardinal allowed Galileo to continue researching his theory so long as he never claimed it was a scientific *fact*. Galileo had to qualify that he was only speaking hypothetically. He initially agreed to these terms, but sixteen years later, Galileo published a book defending the Copernican view as scientific fact. That got him in hot water.

By now, I hope you have noticed how the warfare narrative oversimplifies and distorts history. Yes, the religious establishment saw Galileo as wrong and even dangerous, but it was not because they saw him as rejecting the Bible or Christianity. He was never tortured, and he did not spend a day in jail. Contrary to popular belief, Galileo was not an atheist, nor was he named a heretic. Galileo the scientist actually cited Scripture extensively to support his views, and he remained a Roman Catholic to the end of his days.

Our assumptions about the Scopes Monkey Trial misrepresent history in similar ways. We have formed impressions based on hearsay and movies like *Inherit the Wind*, which itself is based on the 1955 play by Jerome Lawrence and Robert Edwin Lee. Here is how the film tells the story: John Scopes is the hero, the enlightened scientist from 1920s Dayton, Tennessee, surrounded by ignorant, Southern, Christian dimwits. These people are trapped in old, dogmatic ways of thinking. Scopes comes to the rescue by helping them see the light. He is a beloved teacher exposing his students to evolution.

The town leaders are the bad guys in this story, the religious rednecks. They start protesting that Scopes is teaching evolution in the classroom, and they eventually get him thrown into prison. The case goes to trial. On the side of the angels, we have the defense lawyer Clarence Darrow (1857–1938), an advocate for science, reason, and humanity, a man defending the underdog. On the other side, we have William Jennings Bryan (1860–1925), an ignoramus young-earth creationist and an opponent of reason. *Science versus religion, and the winner is . . .*

Once again, this picture is more myth than history. The real situation in 1925 begins with Tennessee passing the Butler Act, which prohibits the teaching of evolution in public schools. The American Civil Liberties Union (ACLU) then places an ad in the *Chattanooga Times*, promising to give legal support to any teacher who will stand trial for teaching evolution. A few enterprising businessmen in

Dayton see an opportunity to gain publicity for the town and boost the local economy. They find John Scopes, a math and physics teacher, who volunteers to teach evolution and be arrested for violating the Butler Act. Indeed, he is arrested, all his bills are paid, and he is immediately released on bail. All of this triggers a media frenzy and a high-profile legal battle. The businessmen have executed their plan to perfection. After all, their whole agenda has been to bring national attention and tourism to the small town of Dayton. Mission accomplished.

As for William Jennings Bryan, he was not even a young-earth creationist! He saw the days of Genesis 1 as long periods of time. He accepted the scientific evidence for evolution but made an exception for *human* evolution; he thought humans were supernaturally created by God. He was especially anxious about how evolution had been used to support the eugenics movement. Eugenicists were trying to perfect the human race by removing mentally and physically defective humans from the gene pool. Bryan accepted the science of evolution but rejected its eugenics application.

In the Scopes Trial mythology, Bryan and his fellow fundamentalists lost. They were roundly defeated by the defenders of truth and science. But that certainly was not how people reacted at the time of the trial. Newspaper articles could not decide the case either way. And when Bryan died unexpectedly five days after the trial, he became a hero overnight. Millions of people adored him. According to one account,

> Crowds lined the railroad track as a special train carried his body to Washington for burial at Arlington National Cemetery. Thousands filed by the open casket, first in Dayton, then in several major cities along the train route, and finally in the nation's capital. America's political elite attended the funeral, with senators and cabinet members serving as pallbearers. Country music ballads picked up the lament while fundamentalist leaders competed to carry on Bryan's crusade against teaching evolution.[6]

It is striking how much popular mythology differs from history.

If you have read anything by Christopher Hitchens, Sam Harris, or Richard Dawkins, then you know the conflict myth is alive and well. They have published books with notoriously feisty titles like *God Is Not Great: How Religion Poisons Everything* (Hitchens); *The End of Faith: Religion, Terror, and the Future of Reason* (Harris); and *The God Delusion* (Dawkins). These authors, dubbed the New Atheists, are relentless and often bombastic in their critique of religion. They hold up science as the shining path to truth, and they condemn Christianity as the worst thing since the Bubonic Plague. Dawkins, for example, is an evolutionary biologist and a retired professor of science at the University of Oxford. Listen to what he said about religious explanations during a 2013 debate at Cambridge with Rowan Williams, the archbishop of Canterbury at the time:

> [Religion is a] cop-out: a betrayal of the intellect, a betrayal of all that's best about what makes us human, a phony substitute for an explanation, which seems to answer the question until you examine it and realize that it does no such thing. Religion in science is not just redundant and irrelevant, it's an active and pernicious charlatan. It peddles false explanations, or at least pseudo-explanations, where real explanations could have been offered, and will be offered. Pseudo-

explanations that get in the way of the enterprise of discovering real explanations. As the centuries go by religion has less and less room to exist and perform its obscurantist interference with the search for truth. In the 21st century it's high time, finally, to send it packing.[7]

At this point, you may wonder who masterminded this warfare metaphor. Where did it come from? Historians blame two influential books from the nineteenth century: John Draper's *History of the Conflict between Religion and Science* and Andrew White's *A History of the Warfare of Science with Theology in Christendom*.[8] (Again, the book titles are a dead giveaway.) These two books created the myth that science and religion are in endless conflict. John William Draper (1811–1882) was one of the founders of the New York University School of Medicine in 1841, when it was known as the University Medical College. He served as the faculty president from 1850 to 1873. Andrew Dickson White (1832–1918) was one of the founders of Cornell University and served as its president from 1866 to 1885. Both Draper and White claimed science was in a war against religion, and science was winning. Religion was on the retreat; defeat was imminent. Surrender or die.

Based on what we have seen in the stories of Galileo and the Scopes Monkey Trial, I hope you are starting to question this warfare metaphor. There is still more to say, of course, but the picture of a persistent conflict between science and faith is bad history. When we revisit the past to look at *actual* scientists and *actual* theologians, when we observe what they thought and said about science and faith, we discover that science and Christianity have had a more complex relationship—diverse, subtle, surprising, tangled, and messy. Thus, it is misleading to claim science and faith are perpetually at war. Their interaction in history is not merely one of conflict and tension.[9]

Christian Assumptions Make Science Possible

Before drilling deeper into that history, let me first clarify what I mean by the word *science*. The word derives from the Latin for knowledge: *scientia*. Sometimes scientific knowledge is broadly defined to include a range of disciplines. In Germany, for instance, science (*Wissenschaft*) is not limited to the natural sciences but includes the social sciences and humanities. But when I use the term, I don't mean *social sciences*, like psychology, sociology, linguistics, economics, or political science. Rather, this book is focused on the "hard" or *natural sciences*, disciplines like physics, chemistry, and biology.

But how do we know what counts as a natural science and what does not? Philosophers who specialize in defining terms like *science* have struggled to find a tight answer. Is acupuncture in or out? What about psychokinesis or alternative medicine? Some spend careers studying unidentified flying objects (UFOs), or unidentified aerial phenomena (UAP). Is this kosher research or snake-oil science? Answering such questions is surprisingly complicated.[10] For our purposes, let us say natural scientists are men and women who investigate the natural world empirically, objectively, and rationally.[11]

The Meaning of the Word Science

Scientists engage creation *empirically* rather than *philosophically*; they seek knowledge through sense experience. Yet this distinction between empirical and philosophical research is relative, not absolute. Scientists are not *merely* empirical in their research; they come to their work with theological and philosophical assumptions. They (even atheists!) interpret the empirical data using broad conceptual and philosophical categories. Though philosophers and scientists have similarities, they use distinct tools and emphasize distinct aspects of creation. Scientists go out in nature to study its inner mechanisms—looking at cells under a microscope, conducting clinical trials on a new emphysema drug, or studying rock samples in Yosemite National Park to uncover past geological processes. Scientists are empirical when they make observations, gather data, and carry out experiments others can reproduce.[12]

Good science also aims to be *objective*. Any valid scientific theory must be objective in how it sorts through the empirical data rather than simply cherry-picking. Here is one example of science failing to be objective: Physicians in the nineteenth century thought they could identify human personalities by bumps and depressions on people's skulls. This approach, called phrenology, was hailed as the future in fighting crime, but it was eventually discredited. The problem was that scientists were interpreting the data in a highly selective way. There was no real objectivity. The scientists zeroed in on physical data supporting their theory and ignored the rest. Conversely, good science tries to be as objective as possible by weighing *all* the available evidence.

Finally, not just any interpretation of the physical evidence will do. Scientific theories should have a *rational* connection to the data. Astrology, for example, claims we can predict world events by studying the positions of stars and planets. Ronald Reagan's wife, Nancy,

> regularly consulted a San Francisco astrologer, Joan Quigley, for guidance while in the White House, relying on Quigley's astrological advice to such an extent that it affected timing of presidential speeches, appearances, meetings with heads of state, airplane travel schedules, and even discussion topics.[13]

I wonder how Reagan's vice president, the cabinet, and the White House staff would have reacted, had they known. They would have been shocked, surely, and rightly so, since there is no rational connection between Reagan's life and the movement of celestial bodies. Quigley's astrology was pseudoscience.

Theological Foundations of Science

Now that we have a clearer sense of what science is, we can see why Coyne and flat-earthers are wrong. Far from being antithetical to faith, it turns out Christian assumptions about creation make science possible. For one thing, Christianity assumes that animals like seahorses, koalas, and flamingos are part of God's creation rather than being part of God's nature, that animals and their ecosystems are real and separate from the divine nature. Sometimes called the *Creator-creature distinction*, this assumption provides the basis for reliable science. Historically, many people have believed creation is divine. Pantheists, for instance, teach that nature is divine and thus sacred. But if we believe nature is divine, then we would be less likely to investigate it empirically, lest we blaspheme God. The pantheistic outlook would lead us to pursue spiritual, not empirical, explanations for natural phenomena. In fact, science emerged in Europe in large part because Christians recognized that nature is not divine.

Furthermore, Christians affirm the fundamental goodness of creation. This belief that creation is good implies that it has intrinsic value and is worthy of empirical study.

DOES SCIENCE MAKE GOD IRRELEVANT?

The theological assumption that creation is good was instrumental in the development of science in the West (whether scientists today recognize it or not). Many people in history, such as the ancient Greek Gnostic philosophers, had a very different view of creation; they thought that physical matter is evil—only *spiritual* reality is good. Nothing like empirical science could have developed in a Gnostic culture. Thankfully, Christianity operated by a different logic.

Irenaeus, the third-century church father, blew the whistle on Gnosticism, arguing that since the eternal Son took on human flesh, we should never disparage the physical creation. For him, the incarnation proves the goodness of matter. Better yet, Irenaeus argued, Jesus not only was incarnate but rose again from the dead bodily. In this way, the Son of God bound himself to creation forever. Jesus is embodied even now in his heavenly session at the Father's right hand, and he will be embodied when we see him face-to-face in the new heavens and new earth. Because of these gospel truths, early Christians were convinced that nature is deeply valuable and worthy of study. And their belief in the goodness of matter paved the way for the Scientific Revolution in the seventeenth century.

Scientific inquiry also owes much to the Christian assumption that creation is knowable, rational, and dependable. These facts about our world make the most sense in a theistic framework where the underlying coherence of creation mirrors God's wisdom. In ancient cultures, the cosmos was seen as chaotic, changing at the whim of testy gods who might zap you when angry. The Christian view of the world is not like that at all; creation itself has an intrinsic rationality that derives from God. Scientists like René Descartes (1596–1650) and Isaac Newton believed that "laws of nature" describe regularities originating from God's mind. Samuel Clarke, one of Newton's allies, wrote that the "course of nature, truly and properly speaking, is nothing else but the will of God producing certain effects in a continued, regular, constant, and uniform manner."[14] Remove the Christian God from the equation, and science reduces to a set of laws without a lawgiver.

Worse yet, without God, the existence of real scientists would be impossible to explain, people like Marie Curie, Albert Einstein, and Stephen Hawking. Their capacity to think rationally, draw connections between things, and examine facets of the physical world—all of it would be deeply mysterious. Where did these genius minds get their abilities? The standard answer is that our cognitive capacities emerged from a long evolutionary process. But how could we trust our scientific observations if we do not know that our cognitive abilities evolved to discover *truth* about the world? What if they evolved unreliably? Christians have a good reason to trust empirical observations. In our view, science is possible because God made humanity *in his image*. It makes all the difference in the world, for truth itself is grounded in God; "the Lord is the true God" (Jer. 10:10), and his very words are truth (John 17:17). The human mind's bent toward truth reflects God's mind.

One of the most striking examples of a Christian doctrine that encouraged the rise of modern science is the fall of Adam and Eve. I'm not kidding. Science developed in part because of the belief that sin entered the world through Adam.[15] Let's pick up the story from Reformers like Martin Luther, John Calvin, and Ulrich Zwingli, who affirmed this doctrine. They believed that humanity participated in Adam's first sin in the garden of Eden. That sin corrupted the whole human race, and now each of us comes into the world morally tainted. According to the Reformers, the effects of Adam's sin extend all the way down to our *cognitive* faculties, rendering them unreliable on their own.

This idea would turn the world upside down. Consider how it affected Francis Bacon, a scientist in the seventeenth century. Since sin corrupted our mental faculties, Bacon distrusted philosophical conclusions drawn from first principles rather than observation. Instead, he valued the powers of observation, investigation, measurement, and gathering data—the empirical method—arguing that trustworthy conclusions are possible only if we investigate the world directly—that is, if we practice empirical science. Other scientists in the seventeenth century shared Bacon's inductive approach.[16] In a nutshell, that is how belief in Adam's fall contributed to the rise of empirical science.

If you pause for a minute to think about it, it is not so strange that theological assumptions played a key role in how we do science today. Modern science grew out of a European culture steeped in the Judeo-Christian faith. Many early scientists were fully committed to *natural theology*. They believed that studying nature helps us discern the very wisdom of God. They were routinely trying to prove God's existence and attributes by studying his creatures and the natural world. As the botanist

John Ray (1628–1705) wrote, "There is for a free man no occupation more worthy and delightful than to contemplate the beauteous works of nature and honour the infinite wisdom and goodness of God."[17] Science and theology are cousins from the same extended family. Most of the sixteenth- and seventeenth-century scientists hailed from European nations like Italy, England, Germany, and France—many of them Roman Catholics or descendants of the Protestant Reformation. Granted, Christianity wasn't the only factor in the rise of modern science.[18] Greek philosophers like Plato and Aristotle played a role, as did Jewish and Muslim thinkers. Nevertheless, we would not have science as we know it without the influence of Christian faith.

Christian Piety of Early Scientists

The plot thickens when we contemplate the piety of early scientists.[19] Here is a list of scientists who embraced Christian theism: Blaise Pascal (1623–1662), Robert Boyle (1627–1691), Robert Hooke (1635–1703), Isaac Newton (1643–1727), Michael Faraday (1791–1867), and James Clerk Maxwell (1831–1879). Each of these men was a notable figure in the history of science. Pascal designed the first mechanical calculator. Boyle gave the famous law we learned in school about the temperature and pressure of confined gases. Hooke was insanely smart and proficient in multiple disciplines, including astronomy, biology, and physics. Newton invented calculus and developed central concepts in classical physics. Faraday discovered benzene and pioneered our understanding of electricity, magnetism, and organic chemistry. And thanks to Maxwell, we know about the laws of electrodynamics. All of these trailblazers in science were fervent believers.[20]

Johannes Kepler (1571–1630) and Maria Sibylla Merian (1647–1717) belong in that great company. Kepler was a German mathematician and astronomer who discovered the three laws of planetary motion. He was also deeply religious, and his theology shaped his scientific research. Kepler was obsessed with the Trinity and would often invoke the Father, Son, and Holy Spirit while working on the movement of the planets. His book *The Harmony of the World* is full of hymnody and prayer. As a young man, he studied theology at the University of Tübingen, in Germany. But years later, he wrote to a former professor: "I had the intention of being a theologian. For a long time I was restless: but now see how God is, by my endeavors, also glorified in astronomy."[21] Kepler died at age fifty-eight after a life filled with tragedy. His first wife died, three of his six children died young, and his mother was accused of witchcraft. Kepler himself endured religious persecution from fellow Lutherans incensed by his heliocentrism. Yet, even on his deathbed, he was confident in the hope of his salvation: He relied "solely on the merit of our savior Jesus Christ, in which is founded all refuge, solace, and deliverance."[22]

Most people have never heard the name Maria Sibylla Merian.[23] That's because female scientists in the seventeenth century were unheralded and unlikely to become household names. But Merian's remarkable gifts set her apart; she was obsessed with insects. From the age of thirteen, Merian studied silkworms in her hometown of Frankfurt am Main. She then moved on to collecting caterpillars to observe their transformation by metamorphosis into gorgeous butterflies and moths. Merian became proficient at illustrating the marvels of nature, depicting flowers and plants and insects in exquisite detail. As one biographer comments,

> Not only was she skilled in watercolor and oils, in painting textiles and engraving copperplates; not only could she render flowers, plants, and insects with perfect naturalness; but she also was a knowing observer of the habits of caterpillars, flies, spiders, and other such creatures.[24]

While other women in that era collected insects to render them in still-life paintings, Merian was alone in breeding them, studying them, illustrating them, and then writing up her entomological research in major publications.

As with so many early scientists, the sense of God's presence pervades all of Merian's work. In the preface to one of her first books, she writes:

> These wondrous transformations have happened so many times that one is full of praise for God's mysterious power and his wonderful attention to such insignificant little creatures and unworthy flying things. . . . Thus I am moved to present God's miracles such as these to the world in a little book.

Merian knew to give God the glory for anything she achieved. She went on to write in the same preface, "Do not praise and honor me for it; praise God alone, glorifying Him as the creator of even the smallest and most insignificant of these worms."[25] In the twenty-first century, we don't generally think about entomology in terms of the presence and power of God. Merian would no doubt have countered: *How else could we study the incredible life cycle of insects?*

I hope you now see why anti-science rhetoric is no friend of Christianity. The history of science and its theological assumptions tell a different story. Besides, anti-science shibboleths may preach well to the choir, but no one actually lives that way. Whether we know it or not, we all rely on science in countless ways—when traveling by plane, driving a car, shopping at the grocery store, cooking meals, and just living everyday life. We all live and move in a world mediated to us by insights from science. And that should make us grateful to the Lord. As Kepler wrote, "I give Thee thanks, Creator and God, that Thou has given me this joy in Thy Creation, and I rejoice in the works of Thy hands."[26]

Do not misunderstand my argument. I'm not saying secular scientists are "anonymous" Christians. Many scientists are avowed atheists with no theological bone in their bodies. Yet, ironically, the science they swear by often functions on the borrowed capital of Christianity. While they have detached science from an explicitly Christian framework, its ghosts roam free; deeper theological assumptions haunt them still.

Scripture Is the Elephant in the Room

If not for the revelation we have received from heaven, no one would be debating science and faith. God says things in the Old and New Testaments that are hard, if not impossible, to reconcile with what scientists think about the world we live in. Many Christians past and present have claimed that God made the heavens and the earth only a few thousand years ago. Christians have said that because of Adam's first sin, each of us comes into this world morally bent out of shape, that human wickedness was once so bad, God wiped out the entire human race (and many animals), except for Noah, his family, and the animals on the ark. The Bible claims that God sent prophets, priests, and kings—men like Moses, Aaron, and Hezekiah—who encountered one miracle after another as God set the stage for the coming Messiah. We confess that the Son of God became incarnate, lived a righteous life, died unjustly, and then rose again for our salvation. But most of these beliefs contradict prevailing scientific accounts of history and the natural world. As a result, many Christians perceive science as a threat to biblical faith. They are mistaken. *Scientism* is the real threat, not science.[27]

God and Scientism
Francis Crick, who won the Nobel Prize in 1962 for his role in discovering the double helix structure of DNA, said this about human beings:

> Your joys and your sorrows, your memories and your ambitions, your sense of personal identity and free will, are in fact no more than the behavior of a vast assembly of nerve cells and their associated molecules.[28]

This insight became his "astonishing hypothesis."

Consider what this means. If Crick is right, we can only understand ourselves through biology and chemistry. Crick's position is called *scientism*. It is the view that *only* the hard sciences have access to true reality, that disciplines like physics, chemistry, and biology give us the only reliable knowledge of ourselves and the world. Advocates of scientism say that the claims of philosophy and theology are less trustworthy because they are not empirical or testable like the natural sciences. At its most extreme, scientism teaches that, in principle, nonscientific claims cannot be true.

The problem with scientism is that many things we know to be true cannot be proved scientifically. Take any historical event, like the Holocaust. It is not scientifically testable, but we believe the abundant evidence that has been preserved. We also cannot prove love scientifically, or that sunsets and symphonies are beautiful, but we credit those claims as true. The same holds for spiritual realities: The triune God. Angels. Demons. Cherubim and seraphim. Human souls. Heaven and hell. Miracles. According to scientism, believing in such things is blind faith, not objective truth. Supernatural realities are invisible to empirical science, so for the advocate of scientism, they do not exist. Anyone who holds to scientism will see conflicts everywhere between Christianity and the natural sciences. But this is a false alarm. The conflict is between biblical faith and scientism, not science per se.

One need not be Christian, or even religious, to recognize that scientism is not the same as science. Atheists like Michael Ruse and Massimo Pigliucci, for example, have leveled some of the most incisive critiques of scientism.[29] Scientism is reductionistic, because it ignores parts of reality that are inaccessible to scientific analysis. It is also self-referentially incoherent; scientism does not make sense on its own logic. Its central idea that only the hard sciences give us objective truth is not even provable *scientifically*, so scientism collapses by its own definition. Scientism as a belief system is antithetical to reality as understood by the world religions, including Christianity. A religious person accepts that we cannot properly understand reality apart from nonscientific ways of knowing. Christians, in fact, believe that God's words are more reliable than human modes of knowing.

Scientism also ignores the limitations of scientific research, painting a fairy-tale picture of science that is far removed from reality. Here science is the unassailable truth—"Just the facts, ma'am." My point is not to disparage natural science, nor to rally behind the anti-science movement. I recognize the limits of science, but this does not make me anti-science. I am only emphasizing the limitations of scientific disciplines.

One oft cited paper underscores this point; it concludes that *most published research findings eventually turn out to be false*.[30] How could that be? Several reasons. When studies target a small sample, their research findings are more prone to error. Many scientific papers also include financial, ideological, and other conflicts of interest between the researchers and their results; hence, they often end up being unreliable. The same holds for the newest scientific fields that boast multiple research teams investigating a single question; the pressure to publish prematurely often yields false results. Those are some of the reasons why published research findings end up in the dustbin of history.

Given the history of science, we should not be surprised. The phlogiston theory, for instance, is an idea in chemistry that originated in 1681 with Joachim Becher's book *Physica subterranea* and was later fleshed out in the eighteenth century by German physician Georg Ernst Stahl.[31] The theory stated that every substance has a combustible element, called "phlogiston," which releases when something burns; the more phlogiston a substance has, the more flammable it is. In 1789, Antoine Lavoisier rejected this theory and proposed instead that heat is a gaseous substance—a "calorie"—that flows into objects with a proportional rise in temperature. This became the caloric theory of heat.[32] Both theories made true predictions and were tested empirically, yet they are false by our standards today.

As Thomas Kuhn showed in *The Structure of Scientific Revolutions*, and as others have since confirmed in more nuanced ways, many scientific theories that were once widely accepted have later been rejected.[33] In light of this history, is it not likely that scientific theories we accept today will be replaced in the future? In any given intellectual milieu, scientists embrace theories supported by a strong body of evidence; no one at the time can imagine alternate theories with better explanations of the data. And yet, future theories eventually emerge to replace those earlier theories. These stronger theories were simply *unconceived* at the earlier time. Let's call this dynamic *the problem of unconceived alternatives*.[34]

Now the uncomfortable question: Do scientists today face the same situation? Will theories one day exist that *we just haven't conceived of yet*, theories that explain the data better than our established theories? Even worse: In any given generation, scientists are unable to conceive of the observations, models, predictions, explanations, methods, instruments, and experiments necessary for fully understanding creation.[35] Our present inability to conceive these entities may undermine our ability to understand God's creation scientifically. Perhaps some of these entities are unconceivable *in principle*. Perhaps scientists, in their finitude, are *incapable* of perceiving certain features of creation and its history by natural resources alone.

Science and Anti-Realism

Since every generation of scientists is prone to making mistakes, the history of science exposes the failure of scientism. But if not scientism, what are we left with? Some Christians concerned about conflicts between science and the Bible take an anti-realist approach to science. Anti-realists recognize that any given set of physical data is consistent with multiple scientific theories (that is, *scientific theories are often underdetermined by the data*). So, in this view, rather than offering objective truth about the world, science gives us useful tools for predicting and manipulating natural phenomena. In other words, we never discover the world as it really is, but only as it appears to us.

Christians who feel threatened by evolution, or some other scientific claim, will sometimes take an anti-realist view of the offending theory: "The earth isn't old. It only looks old." In this way, the data no longer threatens faith; crisis averted. But most scientists are not anti-realists about their work. Most scientists are *realists*. They see the aim of science as discovering the truth about the world. When Isaac Newton formulated the law of universal gravitation in the seventeenth century, he didn't think he was merely "predicting" or "manipulating" nature. No, he believed he had discovered a *truth* about the universe. Same with Louis Pasteur (1822–1895) and Robert Koch (1843–1910). According to their germ theory of disease, many illnesses are caused by microorganisms, like bacteria and viruses. Because Pasteur and Koch were scientific realists, they saw germ theory as the sober truth about diseases.

Nevertheless, anti-realists have done us a great service. Their philosophical and historical insights remind us that scientists are fallible. We make mistakes. Our theories fall short. In fact, what the majority of scientists believe in any given period may be false, or only partially true. After all, scientists are finite and fallen like the rest of us. Having said that, I believe Christians should be *realists* about science. We should see one of the central aims of science as discovering the truth about the world. Creation is meaningful because it is the work of the Creator. As John 1:1–3 states: "In the beginning was the Word, and the Word was with God, and the Word was God. He was in the beginning with God. All things were made through him, and without him was not any thing made that was made." Whether they know it or not, scientists are studying the work of Jesus Christ, the eternal Son.

So Christians have good reasons to believe we can formulate scientific theories that correspond to the real world. We accept some form of realism because the world is a created order (objective), humans have been created to work in it (empirical, rational, social capacities), and God in his good providence has ordained the two to go together. We also have good reasons to own up to our human finitude and indwelling sin, the fall's effects on our minds and bodies; this truth encourages us not to claim *too much* for our theories. As Christians, then, our default mode should be to embrace the scientific consensus as an expression of the gifts and limits of creatures made in God's image. This kind of good science is not done in isolation, like it was two centuries ago. Rather, it is collaborative, peer-reviewed, and widely tested before it is accepted.[36]

One caveat though: Christians believe Scripture is inerrant. We hold that God's word is free from any error, not just theologically but historically and scientifically. While we should never treat the Bible as a scientific textbook, we affirm that God has acted in space-time history and that he has said many things in the Old and New Testaments that touch on areas of science. Thus, when we have rightly interpreted what Scripture intends to teach, biblical doctrine can help our scientific investigations. Ignoring biblical teaching when it is directly relevant to scientific research not only dishonors God but also undercuts the realism of our theories. Christians should be skeptical of any elements of the scientific consensus that ignore Scripture's witness.

However, there is an opposite danger to avoid: If we have misunderstood Scripture while claiming it is teaching a truth relevant to scientific investigation *when, in fact, it teaches nothing of the sort*, our faulty conviction will also undercut the realism of our theories. In short, if scientists want to glorify God in their work, they will need God's help. But whatever the pitfalls, doing good science will always be deeply rewarding, a wonderful privilege worth more than its weight in gold.

God and Methodological Naturalism

Here, again, is the dilemma: The Bible describes supernatural realities that seem to conflict with how scientists describe the world. Another common way of handling this conflict is *methodological naturalism*. This practice limits science to the study of *natural* processes only. A scientist operating in accordance with methodological naturalism acts as if only natural entities exist. So, if I am in a lab doing an experiment, I cannot invoke God, angels, or other supernatural entities. I must *do my work as if* (methodological) *no supernatural realities exist* (naturalism). As a believer, I can affirm everything the Bible teaches. I can share the gospel. I can pray regularly and believe miracles happen. But methodological naturalism says that when I am working as a scientist, I must not appeal to such realities. I have to compartmentalize my belief in the supernatural from my work as a scientist.

Methodological naturalism has a stepbrother called *metaphysical naturalism*, the belief that *only natural entities exist*. There is no God. There are no angels. There is no heaven or hell. There are no spiritual realities at all. The only real entities are physical or natural things. This should ring some bells. Metaphysical naturalism is another name for scientism, which is just atheism. *Methodological* naturalists are different; they can accept the reality of a supernatural order, *just not when doing empirical work.*

One reason Christians go along with methodological naturalism is to keep Scripture from being a threat to science. Methodological naturalism merely stipulates that science has nothing to say on supernatural matters; it is agnostic about God, miracles, and other realities that do not fit within the natural, physical order. Christians can believe what the Bible teaches about the unseen realm, but *as scientists* they only focus on the physical world that is open to empirical investigation. This strategy is thought to resolve most perceived conflicts between science and faith.

Another reason to adopt methodological naturalism is the nature of science. Scientists try to discern the natural processes underlying the physical world. Imagine if a scientist always appealed to the miraculous when he couldn't find a natural explanation. What would happen? Reports of miracles would pop up everywhere, and that would spell the death of science. Good scientific research is often painstaking, yields few results, and often raises further questions. Scientists need to persevere in their work, but that would be impossible if they always explained the phenomena they observe supernaturally. Now imagine if scientists proceeded as if God does *not* exist; they would be protected from rushing prematurely to supernatural explanations and from potentially missing real natural processes.

Methodological naturalism is also ecumenical. Scientists who operate in this mode have varied religious convictions, or no religious conviction at all, but despite their differences, they participate in the same shared enterprise. The success of science owes much to the fact that researchers can collaborate in empirical work without getting derailed by metaphysical or theological debate. Whether demons or djinns exist is irrelevant; atheists and religious believers can set aside their religious convictions when doing research. But outside the lab, they're free to believe whatever they want.

Still, some Christians have reservations. They worry that methodological naturalism limits what we can know about the world; scientists using this method will never conclude that God created the world supernaturally, *even though this is true.* That fact seems problematic if the goal of science is to advance us toward a *true* understanding of the world. In the Christian view, science investigates the natural world God created. The Holy Spirit gives us many details in Scripture about what transpired in the distant past, like how the Lord created humanity (Gen. 2:7, 21–22) or parted the Red Sea when he rescued Israel from Egypt (Ex. 14:15–31). We do not have direct empirical access to those events. The physical traces of those events are ambiguous, hard to perceive, or no longer available. Thus, if we want to know everything we can about the world God has made, natural science is an extremely helpful tool, but it is not the only one.

The Christian philosopher Alvin Plantinga argues against methodological naturalism. He says believing scientists should use all they know about the world in their research, facts they know empirically *and facts they know biblically.*[37] When scientists investigate God's creation, including events in the past, they normally study the natural processes of physics, chemistry, and biology. But those natural processes do not exist independent of God. In one of his letters, the apostle Paul writes:

> For by him all things were created, in heaven and on earth, visible and invisible, whether thrones or dominions or rulers or authorities—all things were created through him and for him. And he is before all things, and in him all things hold together. (Col. 1:16–17)

In his ordinary providence, God continually sustains every part of the universe. Even if most scientific work involves nothing miraculous, God is still in the thick of it, holding existence together. However, there will be rare times when God has acted, or is acting, miraculously within a given area of scientific inquiry. Good scientists who are also supernaturalists should always be open to that possibility.

Science and Faith Are Close Allies

If Christianity is true, we must do our scientific work in light of the truth that God reveals himself in creation (*general revelation*) and in Scripture (*special revelation*). We must be scientific realists, not anti-realists; we must be open to God acting supernaturally and not merely operate as methodological naturalists. Above all, we must reject any ultimate contradiction between the order of creation and the witness of Scripture. As the medieval thinkers used to say, God is the author of two books—the book of Scripture and the "book" of nature.

But is that not precisely where Christians get into trouble? We confess that Scripture is breathed out by God and is thus infallible. For this reason, we end up with conflicts between our cherished doctrines and accepted science. To put a fine point on it, are not creationists to blame for manufacturing the irresolvable tensions between science and faith?

When Creationism Gives You a Headache

First, *creationist* is an ambiguous term. We often use it to describe young-earth creationists, who interpret the Genesis creation account literally and believe the earth is six thousand to ten thousand years old. But here I want to use the term more broadly to mean Christians who believe God is the Creator. As Jim Stump observes, all Christians are creationists, but they disagree "about when things were created and whether current scientific theories are correct descriptions of the process of creation or whether they conflict with biblical affirmations on creation."[38] Young-earth creationists tend to handle conflicts between science and faith by resisting the scientific consensus. By comparison, old-earth creationists accept the conclusions of astronomy, physical cosmology, stratigraphy, coral reef study, glaciology, and related fields. Yet they reject macroevolution, especially the evolution of human beings. Meanwhile, evolutionary creationists see minimal conflict between evolutionary biology and the witness of Scripture.

The scientific and theological differences between young-earth and old-earth creationists are weighty, and the differences between both of them and evolutionary creationists are even weightier. We don't have time to sort things out here.[39] The more relevant point is that from the perspective of the majority scientific community, creationists as a whole—and young-earth creationists above all—are not worth taking seriously.

But don't imagine mean-faced biologists cracking their knuckles to beat up on creationists. That would buy into the warfare myth again. Rather the typical scientist is focused on doing good science. Secular scientists often have no overt agenda against faith and couldn't care less about creationists' intramural debates.[40] They simply dismiss Christian views of science, especially if they've encountered bad arguments—or bad attitudes—from uninformed believers.

Nevertheless, nonreligious scientists never truly escape the theological context of their scientific work. While they may not be openly hostile to creationists, they are certainly not religiously "neutral."[41] As scientists, they rely on unspoken Christian assumptions. They do science without acknowledging that doing science at all depends on God the Creator and an ordered creation. In fact, they are beneficiaries of God's common grace.[42] Scripture also tells us they are actively suppressing general revelation (Rom. 1:18–23). The bottom line: Western bias toward scientism has created persistent tension and controversy between mainstream scientists and creationists.

The intelligent design movement is controversial in academia because of its central thesis that the origin of some features of nature requires a mind—an intelligent designer. This movement emerged after Phillip Johnson's book *Darwin on Trial* exploded onto the scene in 1991.[43] Michael Behe made the case for "irreducible complexity" in *Darwin's Black Box* (1996), and William Dembski defended concepts like the "design filter" and "specific complexity."[44] Since the intelligent design movement focuses on scientific rather than religious arguments, young-earth and old-earth creationists can work alongside atheists, agnostics, and evolutionists who embrace the design thesis.[45]

But here is what is most striking about these approaches: *none of them assume science and faith are incompatible*. Even the most ardent young-earth creationist believes Scripture is wholly consistent with natural science.[46] Aside from their different convictions about the age of the earth and human origins, creationists have other beliefs that diverge from the scientific consensus, like the belief that humans have souls and that God performs miracles. Creationists are not rejecting science outright; rather, they question particular scientific *interpretations* of the physical evidence.

Well and good, yet many scientists still dismiss young-earth creationists as prime examples of scientific denialism. They lump young-earthers in with flat-earthism and other wild conspiracy theories. Many see Christians who reject evolution as ostriches with their heads in the sand, denying the facts and encouraging post-truth disinformation. But such judgments are uncharitable and too hasty. To be sure, young-earth creationists usually resist reinterpreting Scripture to resolve conflicts between science and faith. In their view, whenever our best science and core doctrines conflict, Christians must prioritize what the Bible teaches.

Regardless of what we think of the young-earth position, it's important to see why disagreeing with the consensus on the age of the earth or evolution can be a rational thing for Christians to do. After all, how do scientists arrive at the belief that the earth is old, or that evolution happened? They examine physical data, carry out experiments, and then draw inferences about the distant past. For example, they look at tree rings to infer past climate conditions, or study fossils to infer the evolution of species over millions of years. These scientific claims about the remote past are based on *indirect* empirical evidence; scientists are drawing historical inferences from the empirical data.

Make no mistake, this kind of inferential reasoning is a perfectly legitimate mode of science. But compared with scientific claims based on *direct* empirical data, historical scientific inferences are more prone to error. Such inferences work at a higher, complex level that coordinates different theoretical ideas. As a result, they are more likely to carry unrecognized religious and philosophical baggage. In other words, claims by the historical sciences are less certain and more open to critique. Given the biblical testimony and the structure of Christian theology, young-earth believers are fully rational in their disagreement with an old-earth view, and in their conviction that God created a functional universe in six days.[47]

By contrast, flat-earthers are indeed irrational; they deny direct empirical evidence from our God-endowed senses; the earth's spherical nature *is empirically verifiable*.[48] Conspiracy theories are pernicious because they reject direct empirical evidence. Proponents of such misguided views essentially deny that "which we have heard, which we have seen with our eyes, which we looked upon and have touched with our hands" (1 John 1:1). God gave us our five senses as a normal, rational mode of interacting with the world he created. Assuming I am functioning normally—my brain is not damaged, I am not hallucinating, and so on—I should trust what my senses are telling me. That is the power of good empirical science. This kind of empirical evidence is a special gift from the Creator that we must never carelessly disregard for the sake of our personal beliefs.

When Scientists Behave Badly

The creationist debate sometimes gives the impression that science and faith are always at each other's throats. We saw earlier that history is more complicated. In fact, when we look at the big picture, faith is potentially science's ally. This is especially clear in the field of ethics, where scientific organizations promote ethical and research integrity. Go to entities like the National Institutes of Health (NIH), the National Science Foundation (NSF), or the World Health Organization (WHO), and you'll see careful guidelines and policies for research integrity. Secular scientists know the importance of ethics for a thriving scientific culture.

Consider the infamous Tuskegee study on the natural history of syphilis in African American men.[49] The study began in 1932; the "participants" were 600 black men, 399 with syphilis and 201 without. I use scare quotes because they were not told they were data points in the experiment! And that's not the worst part. These men were left untreated for syphilis for over twenty-five years after treatment was available in 1943. When the study was finally aborted in 1972, a hundred men had died, and others—including their children—had contracted the disease. Thankfully, a class-action lawsuit ended with a $10 million out-of-court settlement in 1974, but no amount of money can redress such an injustice. President Clinton issued a formal presidential apology on May 16, 1997, and modern bioethics came of age by learning from this shameful chapter of medical history.

Speaking of shameful, we should not forget World War II, when Nazi physicians carried out horrific experiments on concentration camp victims. Most of those prisoners suffered brutal deaths, and many others endured long-term physical and mental harm. Closer to home, but equally distressing, is the United States government's treatment of the Navajo miners during the 1950s and '60s. The government covertly studied the effects of radon on the body but did not bother telling the Native Americans that they faced extreme danger from working in uranium mines. Many died prematurely of lung cancer.

Reading about such cases makes the blood boil. They unmask how evil we can be to one another, how we can cavalierly abuse people for scientific gain. The secular scientific community has long been sensitive to such abuses and has taken appropriate measures. We now have institutional review boards for hospitals, universities, and other bodies that do research involving human participants; these committees certify that any research meets high ethical standards. Governments have also enacted legislation to protect the human subjects of research. And scientists now receive extensive training in ethics.

The Christian faith is a friend to such initiatives. For example, humanity's negative reaction to scientific abuses makes good sense when seen in light of Christian theology. Our first parents were made in God's image, and their descendants bear the same divine imprint, with eternity in their hearts (Gen. 1:27; Eccl. 3:11)—no more powerful words have been spoken about the children of men. *Human dignity is rooted in the God who made us.* Given this truth, we rightly respond in horror to any science that violates peoples' intrinsic dignity; we see it as diabolical.

Even with lesser cases of scientific misconduct, biblical faith brings insights that can strengthen secular efforts to promote ethical integrity. In a recent Dutch study of 6,813 researchers, over half of them engaged in suspect research practices such as suppressing negative results, beefing up findings by selective citation, and failing to report flaws in study design. Almost 10 percent of the scientists admitted to falsifying data.[50] These dispiriting statistics reflect the huge pressure to commit scientific fraud.[51] It is tempting to cheat the system if your career trajectory depends on how much you publish, or how many research grants you attain for your university. No wonder they say "publish or perish"!

Every year millions of scientific articles are published. These astronomical numbers hurt the quality of peer review. Think of how many research errors must fall through the cracks; in fact, scientific retractions are becoming commonplace.[52] To make matters worse, scientists must deal with predatory journals that make it easy for busy scholars to publish practically anything. What's the catch, you ask? They charge you substantial sums per article, and they cut corners on peer review. It is a Faustian bargain many find hard to resist. When we take all this evidence together, it points to scientific fraud being widespread and underreported.

The core issue beneath these trends is that *people lack intellectual virtue*. Honesty and humility. Curiosity and open-mindedness. Responsibility and empathy. Scientists without intellectual virtue leave a gaping hole, and scientific abuses come streaming out. It is true that non-Christians have long known the importance of intellectual virtues. Plato wrote about them, as did Aristotle and others in the Greek philosophical tradition. But it is Christians especially who have seen the formation of our minds as not merely academic but uniquely *spiritual*.[53] As W. Jay Wood remarks, the biblical testimony repeatedly urges us to grow in intellectual virtue.

> We are urged to be attentive, wise, discerning, prudent, circumspect, understanding, teachable, lovers of truth, intellectually humble and intellectually tenacious, along with many other positive intellectual traits. . . . On the other hand, warnings abound against laziness of thought, folly, immaturity in our thinking, being easily duped or gullible . . . engaging in idle speculation, intellectual arrogance or vicious curiosity. . . . According to the Christian tradition, to forge virtuous habits of moral and intellectual character is part of what is required for us to grow to the full stature

of all that God intends for humans to be. Becoming virtuous is part of what makes us fit residents of the kingdom of heaven, ready and able to do God's work now and in the age to come.[54]

Take intellectual honesty. When it is in short supply, deceit and fraud flourish. Intellectual honesty is not just telling the truth; it means being an honest person. God created us to be honest, since we bear his image.[55]

Scientific institutions should welcome people transformed by the gospel, people committed to fighting against sin and growing in godliness. Such men and women bear the kind of fruit that nourishes honesty. Nonbelievers are doubtless some of the most brilliant scientists, and they often esteem intellectual virtues and a concern for human dignity. But that is a testament to the providential kindness of God, who sustains and cares for people who do not even acknowledge his existence. Moreover, the intellectual virtues embedded in secular scientific institutions can sometimes be traced back to the residual effects of Christianity.[56] Even people without faith cannot help but testify to their Maker.

When the Universe Is Unimaginably Weird

If you want the real origin story for science, I dare you to read the opening verses of Genesis 1. There we see God as the Maker of heaven and earth; the whole universe is the work of his hands. He spoke the sun, moon, and stars into existence (v. 16). Our finite minds cannot fathom the breathtaking events of the creation week. The Milky Way has between one hundred billion and one trillion stars. By some estimates, the universe has up to one trillion galaxies, which means that between ten sextillion (10 followed by twenty-one zeros) and one septillion (1 followed by twenty-four zeros) stars sprinkle the cosmos. These numbers are mind-boggling—easily more than the number of sand grains on the entire planet, and more than the number of hair follicles on all humans alive today. The limitless wonders of nature and the epic breakthroughs of science make the most sense if this world is the product of God's creative genius. Stating it bluntly: science is obsolete without God.

Cosmologists in the last century practically backed themselves into that conclusion when they realized how uncanny the world is.[57] Our universe is fine-tuned for the presence and flourishing of life. In physics, the four fundamental forces are gravity, electromagnetism, and the weak and strong nuclear forces. Each of these forces has a highly specific value that is crucial for the stability of atoms, compounds, and complex life forms. Had those values been a fraction higher or lower, the universe would have been utterly lifeless.

You may think that is a fluke, but scientists noticed a similar "coincidence" with the mass of protons, electrons, neutrons, and quarks. These tiny particles and their specific weights determine the properties of matter across the universe. Had those values been different by just the slightest degree, then chemistry as we know it would have been impossible. Not just chemistry; *any* kind of life would be impossible. Once again, it is uncanny. This highly improbable fine-tuning, confirmed throughout the universe, has a name: *the anthropic principle*.[58]

The anthropic principle suggests that the universe is a special creation. God is the designing architect. The values are so monumentally improbable that the only sane conclusion is that we are seeing the Creator's fingerprints. Wishful thinking, you say? Hardly. Suppose you came across an Apple Watch while walking on the beach. Is it likely the wind and rain carved out the watch over eons and eons of time? (In the early nineteenth century, the Anglican clergyman and apologist William Paley posed a version of this scenario.)[59] Or take another scenario: An archaeologist stumbles on a cave and discovers a medium-sized box with intricate patterns. Inside are some jewelry and carved figurines. Were these objects formed by natural processes over billions of years? Even asking the question is to flirt with madness. The watch and the artifacts point to skilled craftspeople. In the same way, divine design is the most plausible explanation for the anthropic principle.

Notice what I am not saying. I am not saying the anthropic principle *proves* the existence of God. That would be an overstatement. For some reason, God leaves room for people to deny the evidence that he is the Creator and Lord. Imagine if every day God emblazoned the words *Jesus is the Creator* in flashing neon lights across the sky. Or suppose that whenever any Christians got sick the Lord always healed them miraculously but never did so with non-Christians. Maybe such scenarios would count as "proof," yet God chose to do things differently. He requires *faith*. As Hebrews 11 says, "By faith we understand that the universe was created by the word of God, so that what is seen was not made out of things that are visible"

(v. 3). Faith is the assurance that God exists and acts in the world *even though we do not see him* (v. 1). Without faith, "it is impossible to please [God], for whoever would draw near to God must believe that he exists and that he rewards those who seek him" (v. 6). The anthropic principle is compelling evidence for the Creator, yet we still need faith. But for people who already have faith, the anthropic principle is one more reason to magnify the God and Father of our Lord Jesus Christ.

Here you might object that scientists have discredited many arguments for intelligent design. All it takes is a few minutes with Google to uncover a long line of scientists ruthlessly critiquing the intelligent design movement.[60] In his analysis of the intelligent design position—what he calls born-again creationism—Philip Kitcher writes: "For all the fancy rhetoric, all the academic respectability, all the accusations and gesticulations, born-again creationism is just what its country cousin [young-earth creationism] was. A sham."[61] His critique reflects what many scientists are saying about intelligent design: "It is not scientific."[62] But whatever you think about these objections to the intelligent design movement, arguments from the anthropic principle are not easily explained away. The numbers don't lie; God has left us a remarkable physical trace.

Those who cannot stomach this conclusion appeal instead to the *multiverse* theory. This is the notion that our universe is one of millions of universes. This argument is significant, because if the universe is merely one of a potentially infinite number of universes, then the anthropic principle is no longer an extraordinary coincidence. And if it is not an extraordinary coincidence, says the multiverse theorist, then we do not need to infer a designer God. QED. Problem solved.

Well, not really. Tellingly, there is not a shred of scientific evidence for a multiverse. It is speculation all the way down, smoke and mirrors for brainy people. The theory smells of desperation to avoid the most likely conclusion: science is inexplicable without God.

And, strangely enough, that fits what we know about science. Some areas of science seem impossible to figure out completely. For instance, there is a long-standing debate between quantum physics and general relativity theory. We have experimental evidence for both, yet they seem incompatible. What is going on? In neuroscience, we have the hard problem of consciousness. Scientists and philosophers have puzzled over the relationship between brain and mind, but no one can explain consciousness. In the words of one philosopher:

> Nobody has the slightest idea how anything material could be conscious. Nobody even knows what it would be like to have the slightest idea about how anything material could be conscious. So much for the philosophy of consciousness.[63]

I doubt science will ever solve this riddle. The same inability characterizes other domains of science that are almost unsolvable in principle. Maybe in the future, scientists will figure things out, but it is unlikely. Again, what is going on?

Perhaps God can help us with this conundrum. One of his attributes is incomprehensibility.[64] Since God is the Creator and we are finite and fallen, we cannot understand God fully. Even in the new heavens and new earth, when sin will be no more, we will still not understand God fully. Even after living a billion years as glorified men and women in the blissful presence of God, we will not understand him fully.

> For as the heavens are higher than the earth,
>> so are my ways higher than your ways
>> and my thoughts than your thoughts. (Isa. 55:9)

While God has mercifully revealed himself in Scripture and the created order, most of his nature remains mysterious. We will never understand God fully. Ever.

This fact has implications for creation. Throughout this book I have argued that creation has meaning only with reference to God. Every aspect of creation is related in some way to the Creator. Hence we can fully understand creation only when we have fully understood God. But there is the rub. We can never fully understand God, so why should we think we can ever fully understand his creation? *Since God is fundamentally incomprehensible, his creation is likewise incomprehensible.* As one philosopher aptly writes, "If God's relation to the physical universe is capable of being understood scientifically, then God would be part of the physical universe."[65] It is not that we cannot know anything about the created order. I defended the intelligibility of creation earlier in this book. My point here is that we will never understand creation *exhaustively*.

Even when we fill in gaps in our scientific knowledge, new gaps will emerge, and those gaps will sometimes be inexplicable in principle. We bump up against the same reality that brought Job to his knees:

> Can you find out the deep things of God?
>   Can you find out the limit of the Almighty?
> It is higher than heaven—what can you do?
>   Deeper than Sheol—what can you know?
> Its measure is longer than the earth
>   and broader than the sea. (Job 11:7–9)

In the end, God, the one and only El Shaddai (Gen. 17:1; Job 40:2), powerful beyond measure, is the reason why many scientific questions are irresolvable. Scientists will never fully understand the inner workings of God's world because we will never fully comprehend the almighty Creator.

To God Alone Be the Glory

The question that threads through this book is whether science makes God obsolete. I hope it is now clear why nothing could be further from the truth. Far from being an enemy of faith, science prompts us to deep gratitude to scientists and praise to the living God.

First, gratitude. Reader, cultivate gratitude for scientists. Give thanks especially for scientists who are Christians. Thank them for opening up the beauty, majesty, and brilliance of creation, for helping us see how great God is. Be grateful for all the work scientists invest into uncovering the secrets of the natural world. Join me in offering this prayer for believing scientists everywhere:

> May God's benediction rest on you in every aspect of your research, and may he guide you into all the truth about the created order that he has made accessible.
>
> > The LORD bless you and keep you;
> > the LORD make his face to shine upon you and be gracious to you;
> > the LORD lift up his countenance upon you and give you peace. (Num. 6:24–26)

Second, praise. I hope reading about all these aspects of science leads you to praise the Lord. As you have glimpsed the wondrous complexities of creation, do not resist the impulse to worship the Creator. Science at its best invites us to doxology. Think of the physicians who apply science by bringing healing to billions of people and alleviating some of the effects of Adam's fall. Imagine what the world would be like without surgery, pediatrics, oncology, internal medicine, obstetrics and gynecology, neurology, and the other specialties. Imagine a world without any means of pain relief. Granted, alleviating pain and suffering is not the highest good, and God sometimes allows suffering in our lives to conform us to the image of his Son. Still, modern medicine's ability to heal and relieve suffering is one of God's greatest gifts to humanity. None of it would be possible if God had not made the world *knowable*. Take this time to praise the great physician, all nations! Extol him, all peoples!

We should remember that the Lord is most worthy of praise every time we see the wonders of creation. The sun hanging in the blue sky. A rainbow after a flash storm. Snowflakes falling to the ground, each different from the next. A swallow coasting on the breeze. God's world bursts forth with a thousand marvels that take one's breath away, but that is only what we see with the naked eye.

Science enables us to see deeper layers of stunning beauty, grandeur, and complexity.

The brain has a hundred billion nerve cells, intricately connected to each other, and they allow us to laugh and to cry, to think and to feel, to do everything we take for granted. Right now, the blood in your body includes six thousand million million million hemoglobin molecules, and Richard Dawkins says those molecules are "springing into existence in a human body at a rate of four hundred million million every second, and others are being destroyed at the same rate."[66] Science reveals countless similar facts about the world we live in, exquisite details pointing to the glorious beauty of creation.

The beauty of creation reflects God's infinite beauty. As the psalmist says,

> The heavens declare the glory of God;
> > the skies proclaim the work of his hands.
> > > (Ps. 19:1 NIV)

Any sane person is left in awe and wonder. Even the atheist Dawkins cannot help himself: "The feeling of awed wonder that science can give us," he writes, "is one of the highest experiences of which the human psyche is capable. It is a deep aesthetic passion to rank with the finest that music and poetry can deliver."[67] Dawkins is on the brink of singing the doxology! But he stops short because he thinks there is no Creator. As he says elsewhere, "Although atheism might have been *logically* tenable before Darwin, Darwin made it possible to be an intellectually fulfilled atheist."[68] In the mind of Dawkins, natural selection and evolution can explain everything.

In this book, I have given reasons why I think Dawkins and his allies are wrong. None of the brilliant science they have accomplished would be possible without the God who made them; a fellow can deny oxygen is real, but he will still die for lack of it. Just as breathing is impossible without oxygen, so too science is impossible without God. As surprising as it may seem, science is most at home in the Christian story. Scientists enable us to glimpse the manifold glory of God's world, and that created glory reveals the eternal glory of the Lord of hosts. *Soli Deo gloria*—to God alone be the glory! What can we say in response? We're left stuttering. When words fail us, worship is our best refuge.

Worthy are you, our Lord and God,
> to receive glory and honor and power,
for you created all things,
> and by your will they existed and were created.
>> (Rev. 4:11)

Notes

1. Lawrence C. Hamilton, "Trumpism, Climate and COVID: Social Bases of the New Science Rejection," *PLOS One* 19, no. 1 (2024): e0293059, https://doi.org/10.1371/journal.pone.0293059.
2. E.g., see Asheley R. Landrum, Alex Olshansky, and Othello Richards, "Differential Susceptibility to Misleading Flat Earth Arguments on YouTube," *Media Psychology* 24, no. 1 (2021): 136–65.
3. My thanks to Robert Erle Barham, Phill Broussard, Ken Coulson, Steve Dilley, Paul Garner, C. Ben Mitchell, Tim Morris, Michael Radmacher, Marcus Ross, and Todd Wood for helpful feedback on an earlier draft of this book.
4. Jerry A. Coyne, *Faith vs. Fact: Why Science and Religion Are Incompatible* (Penguin, 2015), xi.

5. For helpful details on Galileo and the Scopes Monkey Trial, see Maurice A. Finocchiaro, "Myth 8: That Galileo Was Imprisoned and Tortured for Advocating Copernicanism," and Edward J. Larson, "Myth 20: That the Scopes Trial Ended in Defeat for Antievolutionism," in *Galileo Goes to Jail and Other Myths about Science and Religion*, ed. Ronald L. Numbers (Harvard University Press, 2009), 68–78, 178–86.
6. Larson, "Myth 20," 185.
7. "This House Believes Religion Has No Place in the 21st Century," Cambridge Union Society, February 3, 2013, https://www.youtube.com/.
8. John William Draper, *History of the Conflict between Religion and Science*, 8th ed. (Appleton, 1884); Andrew Dickson White, *A History of the Warfare of Science with Theology in Christendom*, 2 vols. (Appleton, 1896).
9. For the classic argument along these lines, see John Hedley Brooke, *Science and Religion: Some Historical Perspectives* (Cambridge University Press, 1991).
10. On the demarcation problem, see Larry Laudan, "The Demise of the Demarcation Problem," in *Physics, Philosophy, and Psychoanalysis: Essays in Honor of Adolf*

Grünbaum, ed. Robert Sonné Cohen and Larry Laudan (Reidel, 1983), 111–27.

11. Del Ratzsch, *Science and Its Limits: The Natural Sciences in Christian Perspectives*, 2nd ed. (IVP Academic, 2000), 13. To be clear, I am not implying that the "social" sciences are not empirical, objective, or rational; rather, the natural sciences investigate the natural world, whereas the social sciences investigate human society and social behavior.

12. Not all scientists fit this description—for example, theoretical physics and mathematical physics often address highly abstract and mathematical problems that do not involve any experiments.

13. Haynes Johnson, *Sleepwalking through History: America in the Reagan Years* (Norton, 1991), 453–54.

14. Samuel Clarke, *Truth and Certainty of the Christian Revelation*, in *The Works of Samuel Clarke*, 2 vols. (Knapton, 1738), 2:698, cited in Peter Harrison, "Laws of Nature in Seventeenth-Century England: From Cambridge Platonism to Newtonianism," in *The Divine Order, the Human Order, and the Order of Nature: Historical Perspectives*, ed. Eric Watkins (Oxford University Press, 2013), 143.

15. I am drawing on Peter Harrison, *The Fall of Man and the Foundations of Science* (Cambridge University Press, 2007). For the argument that the Christian belief in divine voluntarism brought about the rise of empirical science, see M. B. Foster, "The Christian Doctrine of Creation and the Rise of Modern Natural Science," *Mind* 43, no. 172 (1934): 446–68; Edward B. Davis, "Christianity and Early Modern Science: The Foster Thesis Reconsidered," in *Evangelicals in Historical Perspective*, ed. David N. Livingstone, D. G. Hart, and Mark A. Noll (Oxford University Press, 1999), 75–95.
16. Philosophers of science today would say that Bacon's inductive approach grossly oversimplifies the actual practice of scientists.
17. Charles E. Raven, *John Ray, Naturalist: His Life and Works* (Cambridge University Press, 1950), 83.
18. For historical nuance, see Noah J. Efron, "Myth 9: That Christianity Gave Birth to Modern Science," in Numbers, *Galileo Goes to Jail*, 79–89.
19. Early scientists were often known as "naturalists," people who studied plants, animals, and other aspects of the natural world, but the word has a different connotation

today. I will use the term *scientist* for these men and women, even if it is slightly anachronistic.

20. Granted, not every early scientist was entirely orthodox in his theology. For example, Isaac Newton was an Arian; he rejected the Trinity. My main point is that many early scientists saw their scientific work as consonant with theistic faith and, indeed, as glorifying to God.

21. Carola Baumgart, *Johannes Kepler: Life and Letters* (Philosophical Library, 1951), 31.

22. James R. Voelkel, *Johannes Kepler and the New Astronomy* (Oxford University Press, 1999), 129.

23. I gleaned her biographical details from Natalie Zemon Davis, *Women on the Margins: Three Seventeenth-Century Lives* (Harvard University Press, 1995), 140–202.

24. Davis, *Women on the Margins*, 140.

25. Davis, *Women on the Margins*, 156.

26. Johannes Kepler, *Weltharmonik*, trans. Max Casper (Oldenbourg, 1939), 350, quoted in Rudolf Haase, "Kepler's Harmonies, between Pansophia and Mathesis Universalis," in *Kepler: Four Hundred Years*, ed. Arthur Beer and Peter Beer (Pergamon, 1975), 526.

27. See J. P. Moreland, *Scientism and Secularism: Learning to Respond to a Dangerous Ideology* (Crossway, 2018).

28. Francis Crick, *The Astonishing Hypothesis: The Scientific Search for the Soul* (Scribner, 1994), 3.
29. See the collection of essays in Maarten Boudry and Massimo Pigliucci, eds., *Science Unlimited? The Challenges of Scientism* (University of Chicago Press, 2017).
30. John P. A. Ioannidis, "Why Most Published Research Findings Are False," *PLOS Medicine* 2, no. 8 (2005): e124, https://doi.org/10.1371/journal.pmed.0020124.
31. My account of phlogiston draws on Ferenc Szabadváry, *History of Analytical Chemistry* (Pergamon, 1966), 45–46.
32. Lin-Shu Wang, *A Treatise of Heat and Energy* (Springer Nature, 2020), 25–26.
33. Thomas S. Kuhn, *The Structure of Scientific Revolutions* (University of Chicago Press, 1962).
34. P. Kyle Stanford, *Exceeding Our Grasp: Science, History, and the Problem of Unconceived Alternatives* (Oxford University Press, 2006).
35. For further elaboration, see Darrell P. Rowbottom, "Extending the Argument from Unconceived Alternatives: Observations, Models, Predictions, Explanations, Methods, Instruments, Experiments, and Values," *Synthese* 196 (2019): 3947–59, https://doi.org/10.1007/s11229-016-1132-y.

36. Given what I have argued above, such scientific conclusions, while well supported today, may turn out in the future to be wrong or only partially true. However, provided there is no conflict with the witness of Scripture and theological commitments, Christians in my view should still support such scientific theories.

37. Plantinga says Christians should pursue "science using all that we know: what we know about God as well as what we know about his creation, and what we know by faith as well as what we know in other ways." "Methodological Naturalism?," in *Facets of Faith and Science*, ed. Jitse M. van der Meer, vol. 1 (University Press of America, 1996), 213–14.

38. J. B. Stump, introduction to *Four Views on Creation, Evolution, and Intelligent Design*, ed. J. B. Stump (Zondervan, 2017), 12.

39. For extended analysis, see Todd Wood, Hans Madueme, and Paul Garner, *Young-Age Creationism: Exploring the Science of Creation* (P&R, forthcoming); Hans Madueme and Stephen Lloyd, eds., *Young-Age Creationism: Restoring the Biblical Metanarrative* (P&R, forthcoming).

40. Anti-religious scientists like Richard Dawkins and Jerry Coyne are not representative of *all* scientists.

41. For example, see Roy A. Clouser, *The Myth of Religious Neutrality: An Essay on the Hidden Role of Religious Belief in Theories*, rev. ed. (University of Notre Dame Press, 2005).
42. For an important treatment of this topic, see Abraham Kuyper, *Common Grace: God's Gifts for a Fallen World*, 3 vols. (repr., Lexham, 2016–2020).
43. Phillip E. Johnson, *Darwin on Trial* (InterVarsity Press, 1991).
44. See Michael Behe, *Darwin's Black Box: The Biochemical Challenge to Evolution*, 2nd ed. (Free Press, 2006); William A. Dembski, *The Design Inference: Eliminating Chance through Small Probabilities* (Cambridge University Press, 1998); Dembski, *The Design Revolution: Answering the Toughest Questions about Intelligent Design* (InterVarsity Press, 2004).
45. If you wonder how an atheist could possibly embrace a designer, the relevant point in this case is that the designer is not a religious deity. Given the empirical evidence of design, such atheists speculate that a natural—not supernatural—designer exists, some even arguing that life on earth originated from aliens. For analysis, see Bradley Monton, *Seeking God in Science: An Atheist Defends Intelligent Design* (Broadview, 2009).

46. In the nineteenth century, for example, creationists routinely attacked "science, falsely so-called"; they saw science itself as legitimate, just not old-earth or evolutionary science. See Ronald L. Numbers, "Science Falsely So-Called: Evolution and Adventists in the Nineteenth Century," *Journal of the American Scientific Affiliation* 27, no. 1 (1975): 18–23.
47. I cannot address all the epistemological issues here, but see a fuller analysis in Hans Madueme and Todd Charles Wood, "Bridging Ideological Divides: Why Christians Still Disagree about Evolution and What We Should Do about It," *Scientia et Fides* 12, no. 1 (2024): 189–213.
48. On the empirical evidence for the spherical earth, we need not belabor the point. We put satellites into orbit based on specific models of the earth's shape and gravity. We see the shape of the earth's shadow on the moon every lunar eclipse. We can circumnavigate, and the shortest distance between two points on earth isn't a straight line. Radio signals can be blocked by the curvature of the earth. We see curvature in large bodies of water—like when we view the Toronto skyline across Lake Ontario. And, of course, astronauts and space probes have seen the earth from space.

49. "The USPHS Untreated Syphilis Study at Tuskegee," CDC Office of Science, January 9, 2023, https://www.cdc.gov/.

50. Gowri Gopalakrishna, Gerben ter Riet, Gerko Vink, Ineke Stoop, Jelte M. Wicherts, Lex M. Bouter, "Prevalence of Questionable Research Practices, Research Misconduct and Their Potential Explanatory Factors: A Survey among Academic Researchers in the Netherlands," *PLOS One* 17, no. 2 (2022): e0263023, https://doi.org/10.1371/journal.pone.0263023.

51. I'm drawing on Marios Stavrakas, Nikolaos Tsetsos, Alexandros Poutoglidis, Aikaterini Tsentemeidou, Georgios Fyrmpas, and Petros D. Karkos, "Fraud and Deceit in Medical Research: Insights and Current Perspectives," *Voices in Bioethics* 8 (2022): 2, https://doi.org/10.52214/vib.v8i.8940.

52. E.g., see R. Grant Steen, "Retractions in the Scientific Literature: Is the Incidence of Research Fraud Increasing?," *Journal of Medical Ethics* 37, no. 4 (2011): 249–53. See also the information gathered at https://retractionwatch.com.

53. W. Jay Wood, *Epistemology: Becoming Intellectually Virtuous* (InterVarsity Press, 1998), 18.

54. Wood, *Epistemology*, 19.
55. Wood, *Epistemology*, 66.
56. For a compelling defense, see Tom Holland, *Dominion: How the Christian Revolution Remade the World* (Basic, 2019).
57. E.g., see John D. Barrow and Frank J. Tipler, *The Anthropic Cosmological Principle* (Oxford University Press, 1986).
58. The literature often distinguishes "weak" and "strong" versions of the anthropic principle.
59. William Paley, *Natural Theology: or, Evidences of the Existence and Attributes of the Deity* (Morgan, 1802).
60. Of course, ID proponents have responded to their critics as well. For a sample of some collected responses, see "Responses to Critics," Discovery Institute, https://www.discovery.org/.
61. Philip Kitcher, "Born-Again Creationism," in *Intelligent Design Creationism: Philosophical, Theological, and Scientific Perspectives*, ed. Robert Pennock (MIT Press, 2001), 287.
62. Mark Perakh and Matt Young, "Is Intelligent Design Science?," in *Why Intelligent Design Fails: A Scientific Critique of the New Creationism*, ed. Matt Young and Taner Edis (Rutgers University Press, 2004), 195.

63. Jerry Fodor, "The Big Idea: Can There Be a Science of Mind?," *Times Literary Supplement*, July 3, 1992, 5.
64. My remarks in this paragraph and the next are indebted to James N. Anderson, "On the Rationality of Positive Mysterianism," *International Journal for the Philosophy of Religion* 83, no. 3 (2018): 291–307, esp. 297.
65. Paul Helm, *The Providence of God* (InterVarsity Press, 1993), 70.
66. Richard Dawkins, *Outgrowing God: A Beginner's Guide* (Random House, 2019), 163. My comment about brain cells is from p. 161.
67. Richard Dawkins, *Unweaving the Rainbow: Science, Delusion and the Appetite for Wonder* (Mariner, 2000), x.
68. Richard Dawkins, *The Blind Watchmaker: Why the Evidence of Evolution Reveals a Universe without Design* (Norton, 1996), 6, emphasis original.

Recommended Resources

Bloom, John A. *The Natural Sciences: A Student's Guide*. Crossway, 2015. This book is part of the Reclaiming the Christian Intellectual Tradition series, which examines academic topics from a Christian perspective. Bloom helps readers understand Christian underpinnings for the practice of science. He shows that far from being a threat to or an enemy of science, the Christian faith was pivotal in science's history, and it is indispensable for clear thinking on current scientific issues.

Keathley, Kenneth D. *Faith and Science: A Primer for a Hypernatural World*. B&H Academic, 2024. Keathley provides a thoughtful exploration of the relationship between science and faith. Drawing from a wealth of theological, historical, and scientific insights, he presents complex ideas in an engaging and accessible manner.

This book is a great antidote for readers who perceive science and Christian faith as adversaries.

Lennox, John. *Can Science Explain Everything?* Good Book, 2019. This brief and highly readable book is perfect for high school and college students looking for a stimulating apologetic resource. Lennox clarifies the limits of science and exposes the problems with scientism as a worldview. He also helps readers think more clearly about the relationship between science and faith.

Numbers, Ronald, ed. *Galileo Goes to Jail: And Other Myths about Science and Religion.* Harvard University Press, 2009. A readable book that debunks a number of common myths about the relationship between science and religion. Each short chapter looks at a different episode in the history of science and religion, separating the historical wheat from the chaff.

Ratzsch, Del. *Science and Its Limits: The Natural Sciences in Christian Perspective.* InterVarsity Press, 2000. An excellent introduction to the philosophy of science. Instead of simply talking past those with whom he disagrees, which is often the case in debates about science and faith, Ratzsch brings conceptual clarity and philosophical insight to many facets of the discussion. After reading this book, your brain will feel like it has gone through a growth spurt—in the best sense!

Wood, Todd Charles. *The Quest: Exploring Creation's Hardest Questions*. Compass Classroom, 2018. Wood writes this book as a young-earth creationist who is passionate about science. Christians are all too familiar with the challenges science presents for faith, questions about whether evolutionary theory can be reconciled with the Bible, or whether Noah's flood was global. Instead of using these hard questions as an excuse to disparage science (or faith), Wood sees these challenges as an invitation to a lifetime of Christian discipleship. In a book that is refreshingly personal, Wood encourages us to engage God's creation with faith, commitment, and endless curiosity.

Scripture Index

Genesis
1 .... 8, 53
1–2 41
1:16 53
1:27 49
2:7 39
2:21–22 39
17:1 60

Exodus
14:15–31 39

Numbers
6:24–26 61

Job
11:7–9 60
40:2 60

Psalms
19:1 63

Ecclesiastes
3:11 49

Isaiah
55:9 59

Jeremiah
10:10 19

John
1:1–3 34
17:17 19

Romans
1:18–23 43

Colossians
1:16–17 40

Hebrews
11 55
11:1 56
11:3 56
11:6 56

SCRIPTURE INDEX

1 John
1:1 46

Revelation
4:11 65

TGC | THE GOSPEL COALITION

The Gospel Coalition (TGC) exists to renew and unify the contemporary church in the ancient gospel by declaring, defending, and applying the good news of Jesus to all of life.

Guided by a Council of more than 40 pastors in the Reformed tradition, TGC seeks to foster a mighty movement of spiritual renewal. We want to see God bless local churches with a gospel-centered ministry that fully integrates corporate worship, expository preaching, joyful obedience to God's Word, effective evangelism, loving community, and faithful engagement in the world.

We do this by producing content (including articles, podcasts, videos, courses, books, and curricula) and convening leaders (including conferences, cohorts, regional chapters, and international coalitions).

Join us by visiting TGC.org.

TGC.org

TGC HARD QUESTIONS

Does God Care about Gender Identity?
Samuel D. Ferguson

Is Christianity Good for the World?
Sharon James

What Does Depression Mean for My Faith?
Kathryn Butler, MD

Why Do We Feel Lonely at Church?
Jeremy Linneman

Where Is God in a World with So Much Evil?
Collin Hansen

Did the Resurrection Really Happen?
Timothy Paul Jones

Does Science Make God Irrelevant?
Hans Madueme

The series TGC Hard Questions serves the church by providing tools that answer people's deep *longings* for community, their *concerns* about biblical ethics, and their *doubts* about confessional faith.

For more information, visit **crossway.org**.